I Love You

Valentine's Day Coloring Book

Color Your Heart, Color your Love

Kimberly Harold

Happy Coloring

Thinking of You

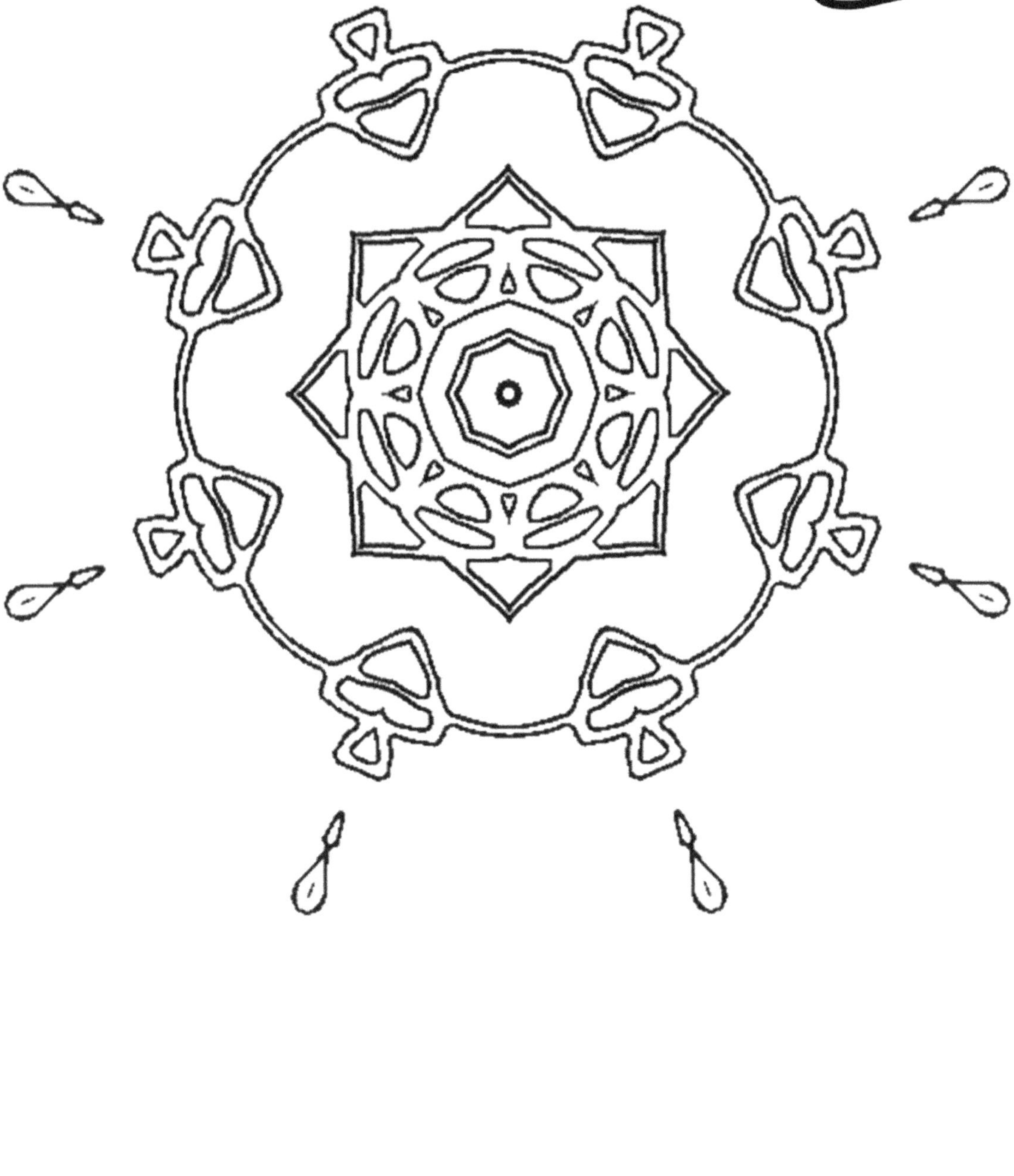

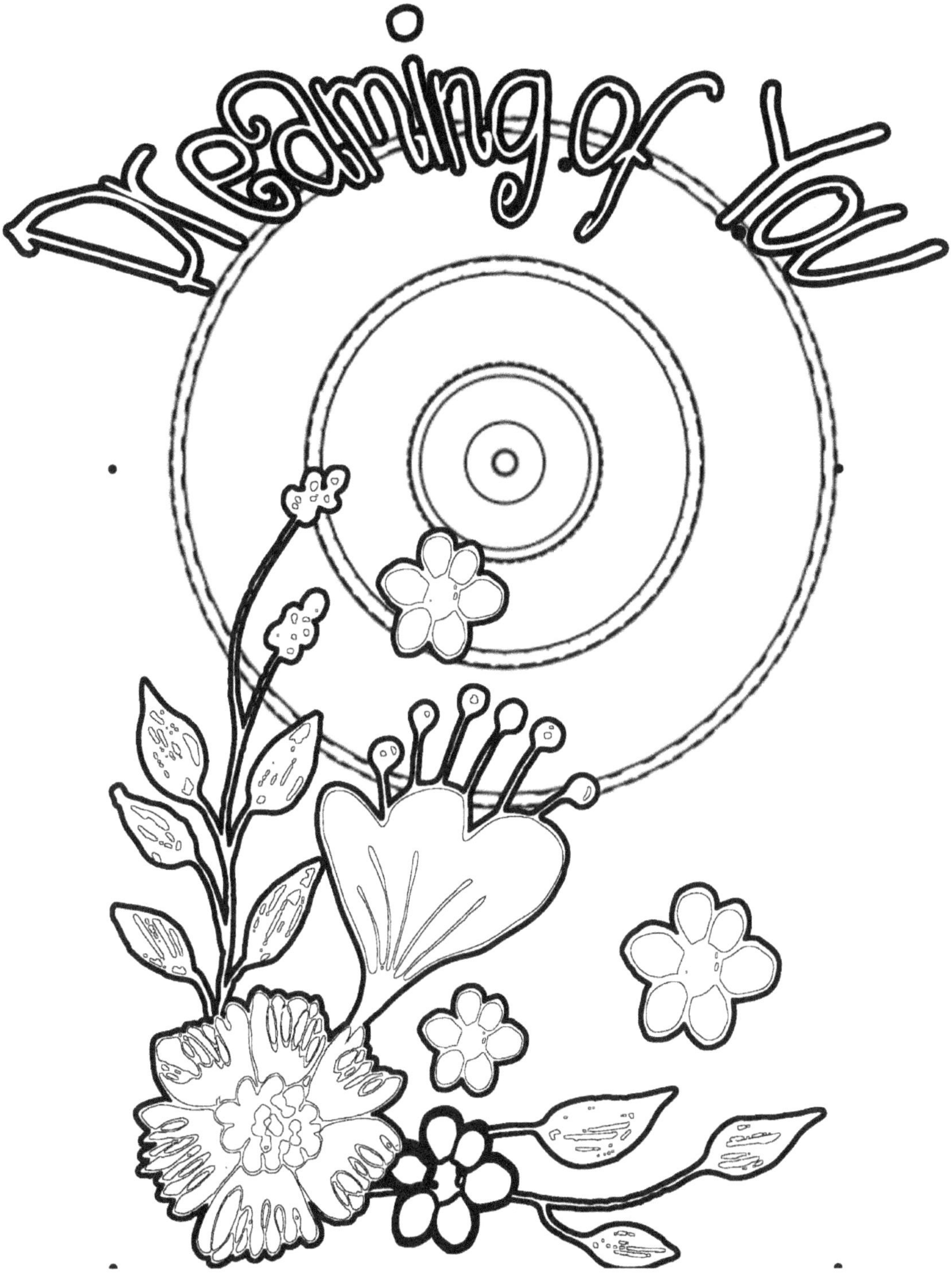
Dreaming of You

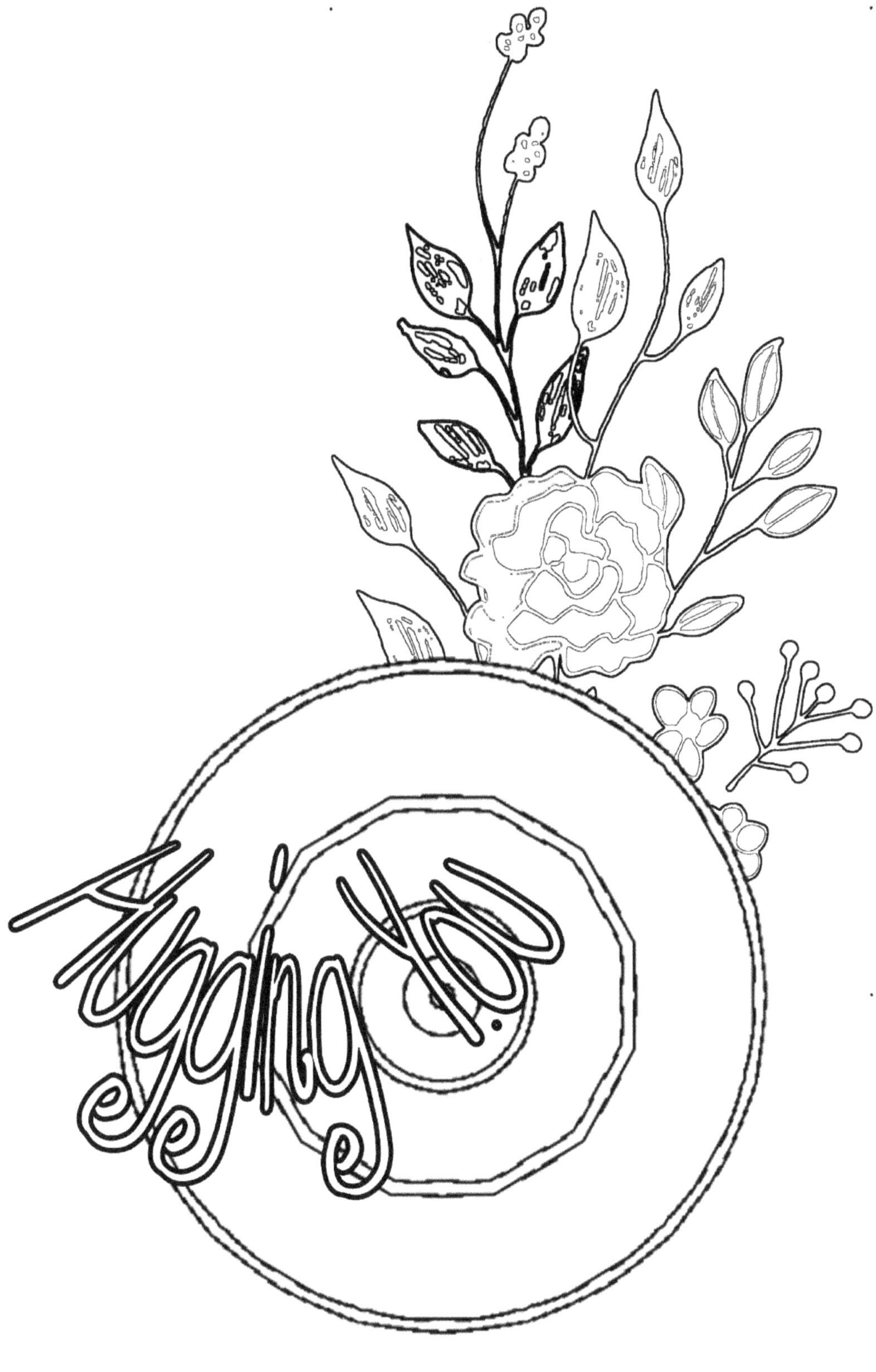
Hugging You

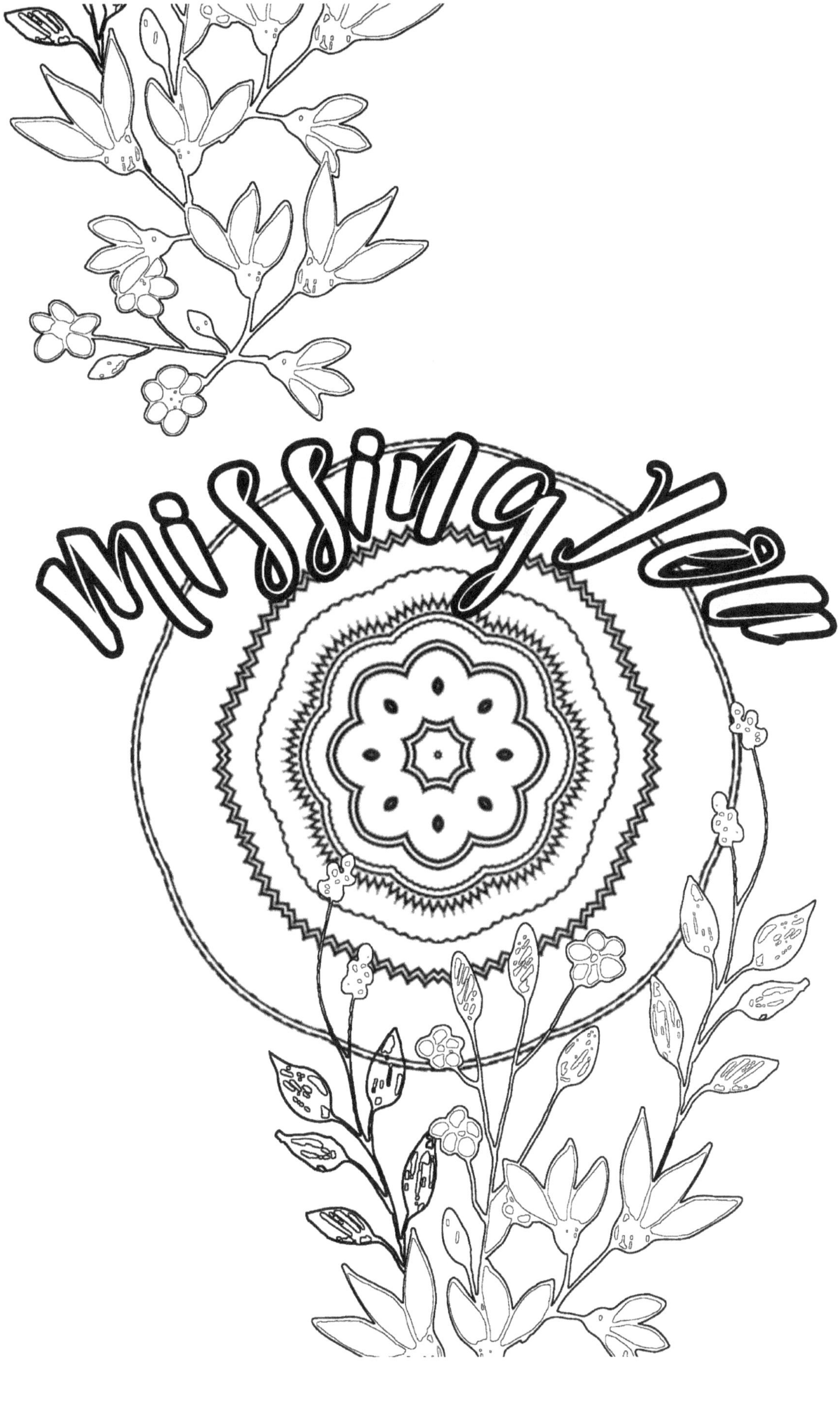
missing you

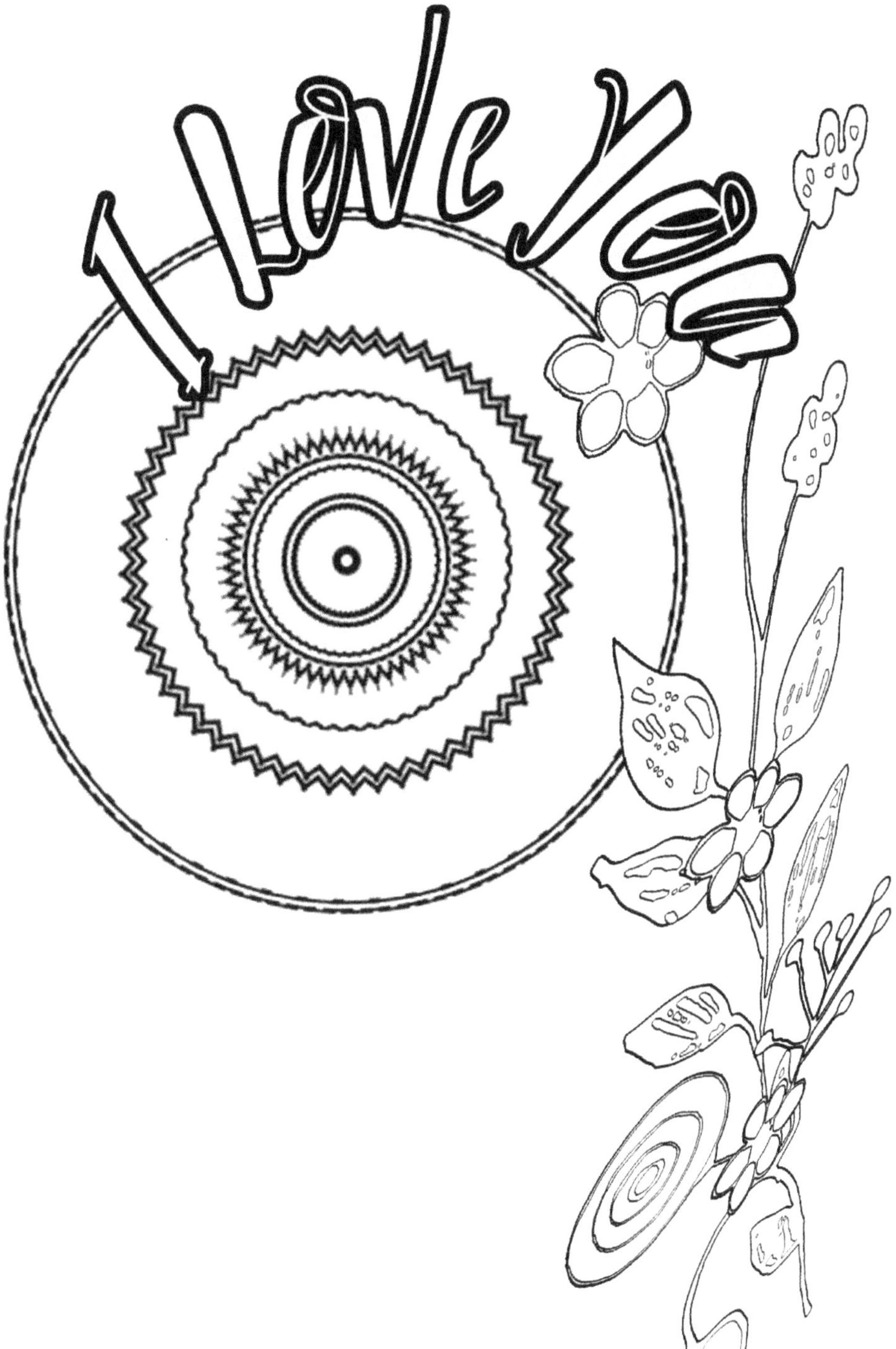
I Love You

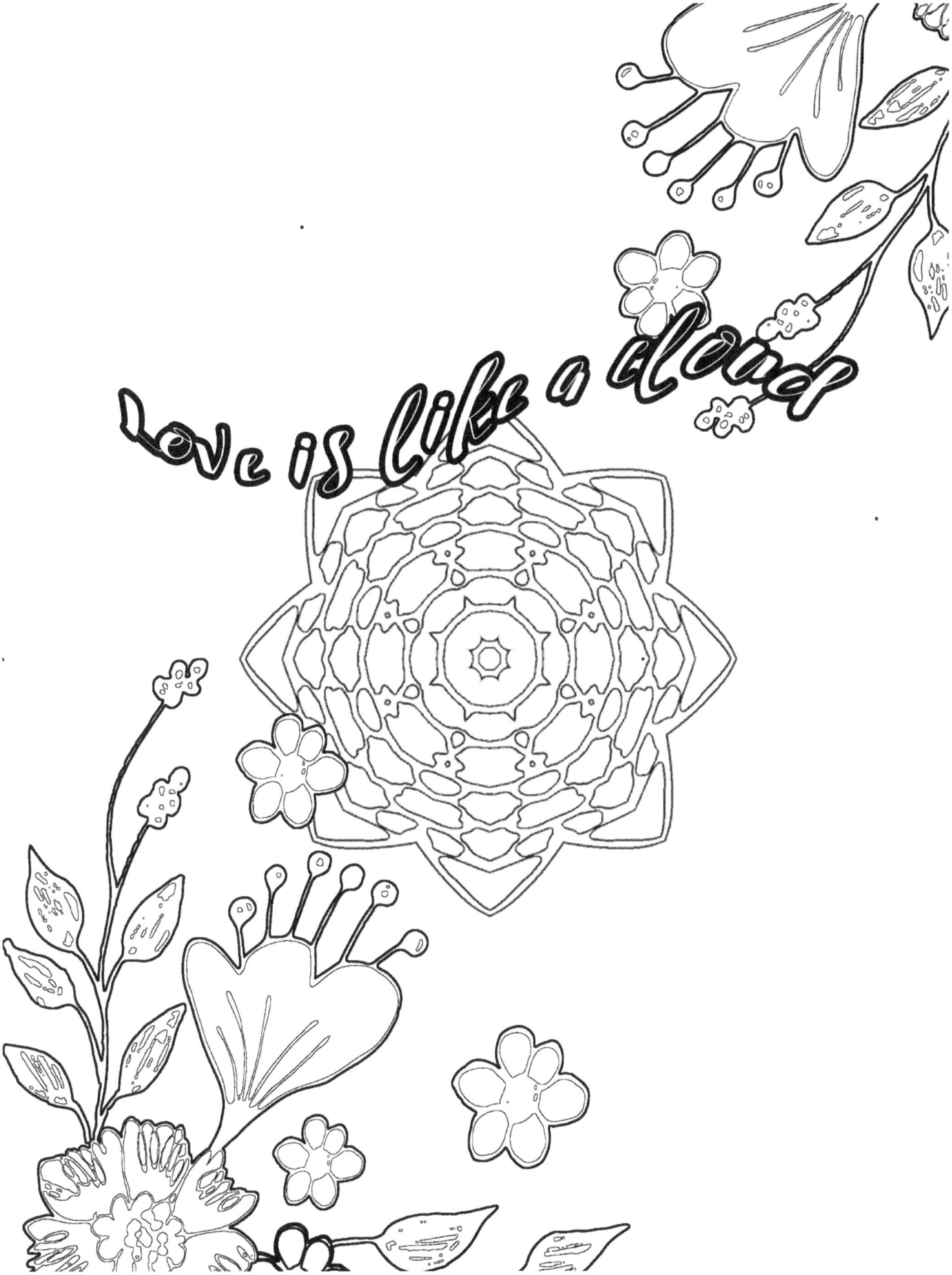
Love is like a cloud

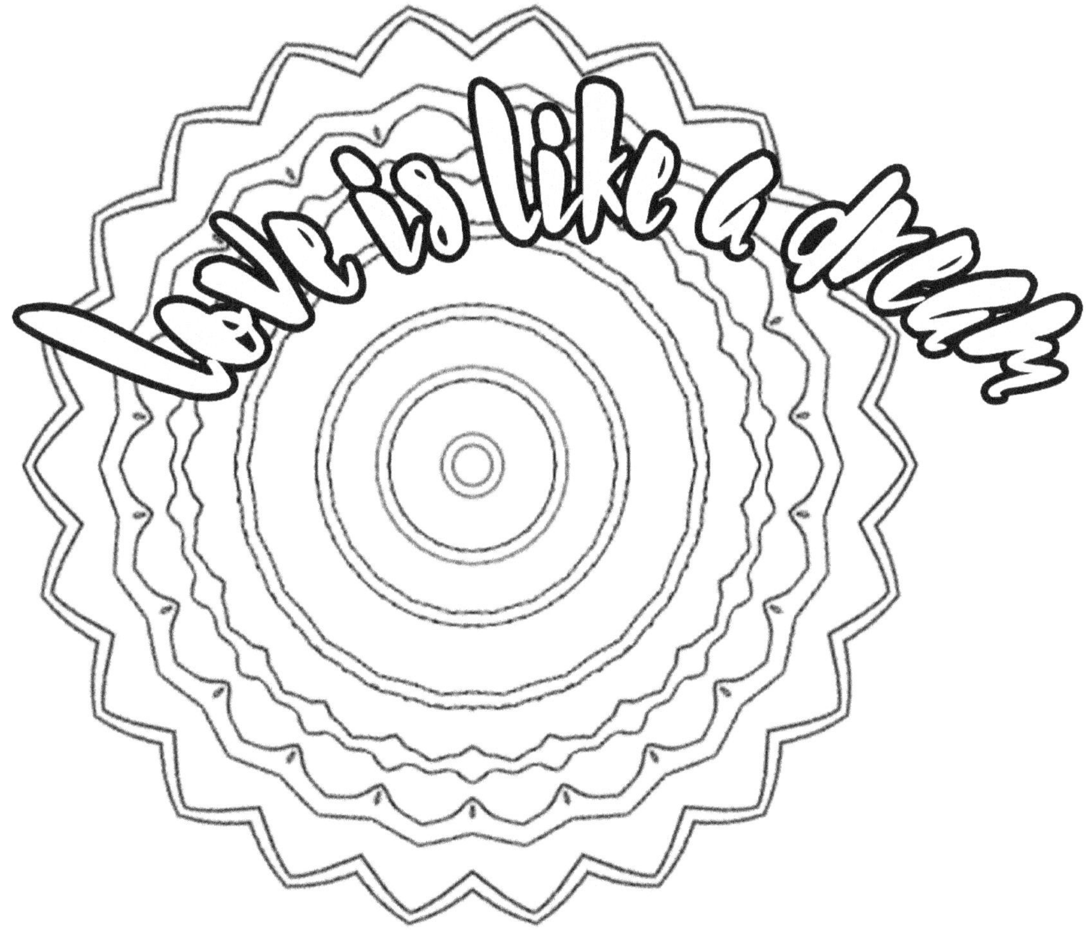
love is like a dream

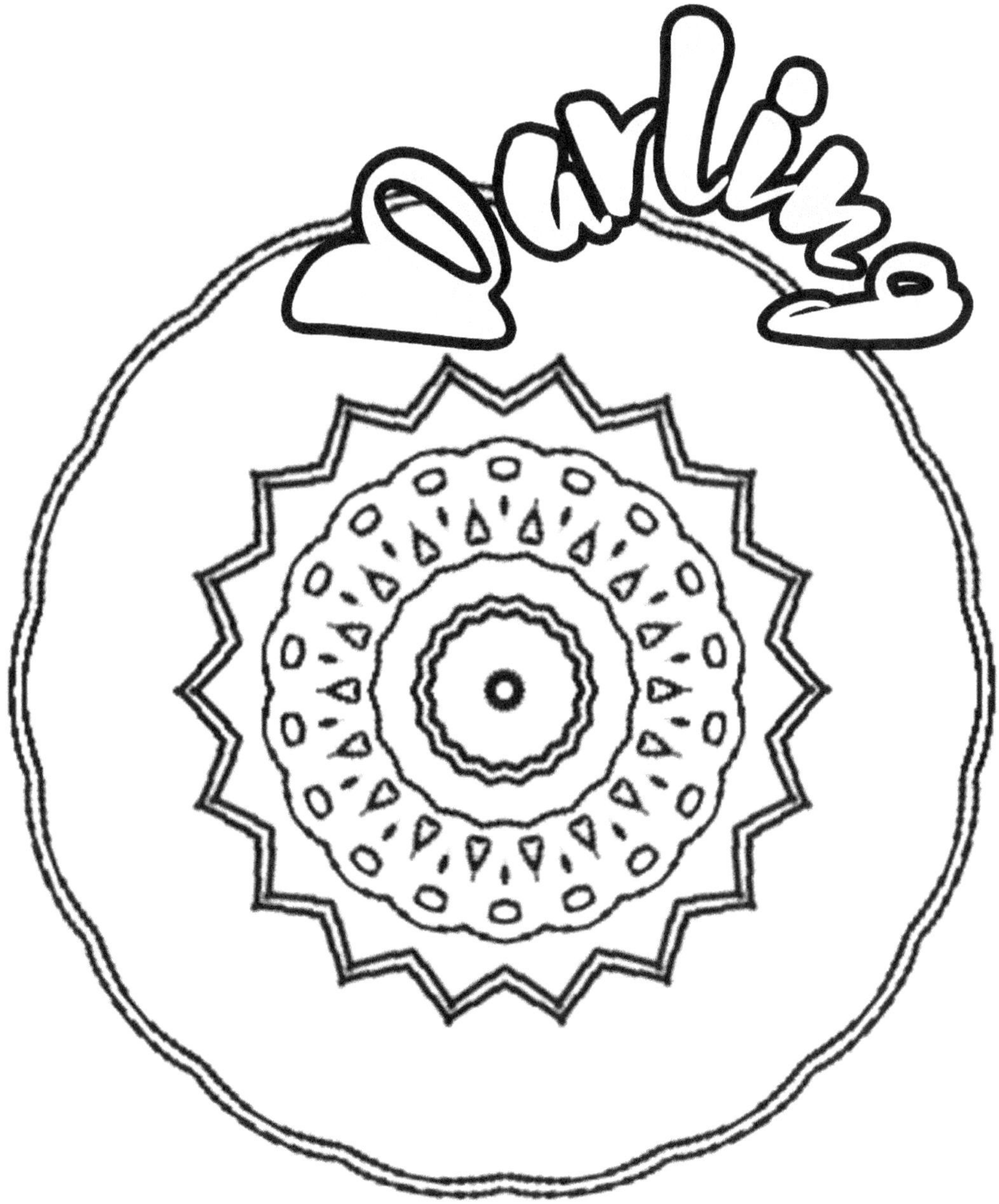
Darling

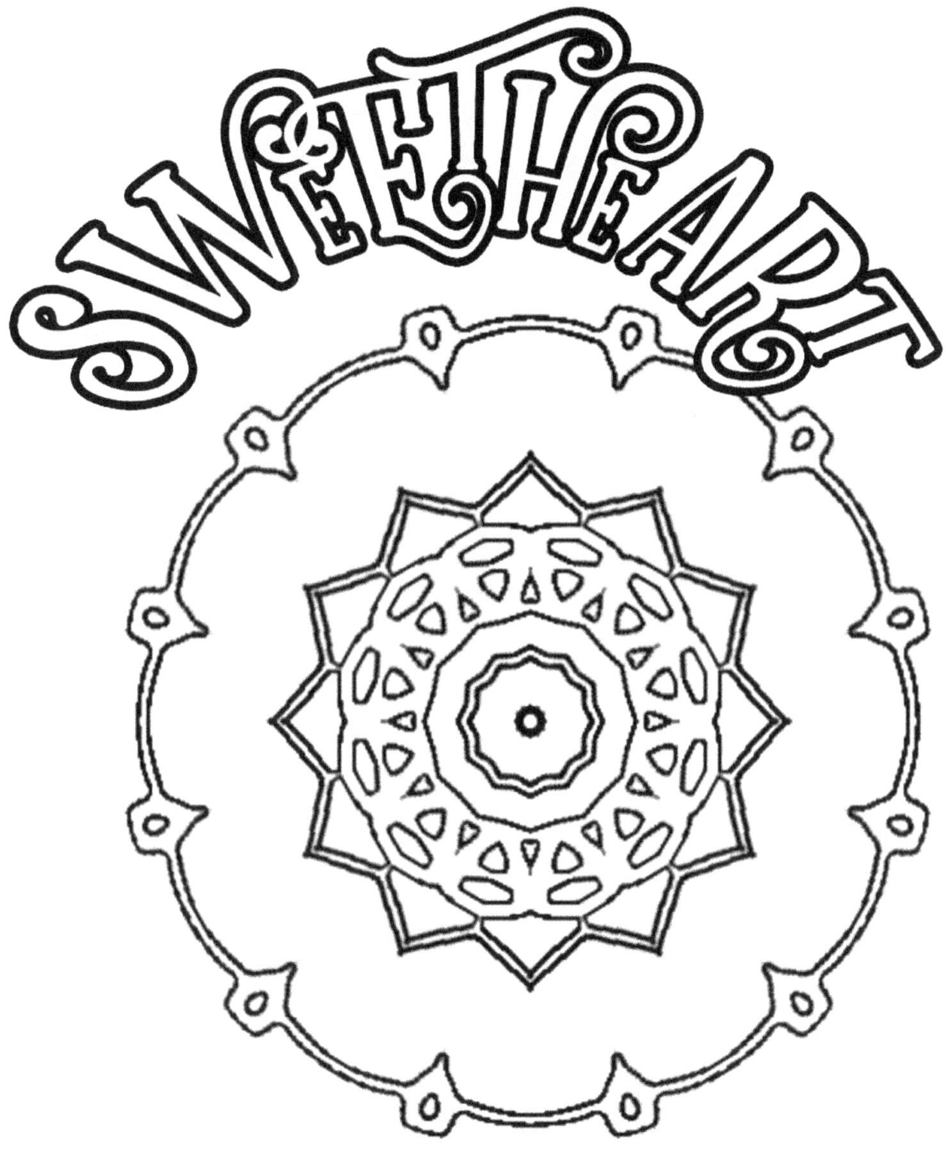
SWEETHEART

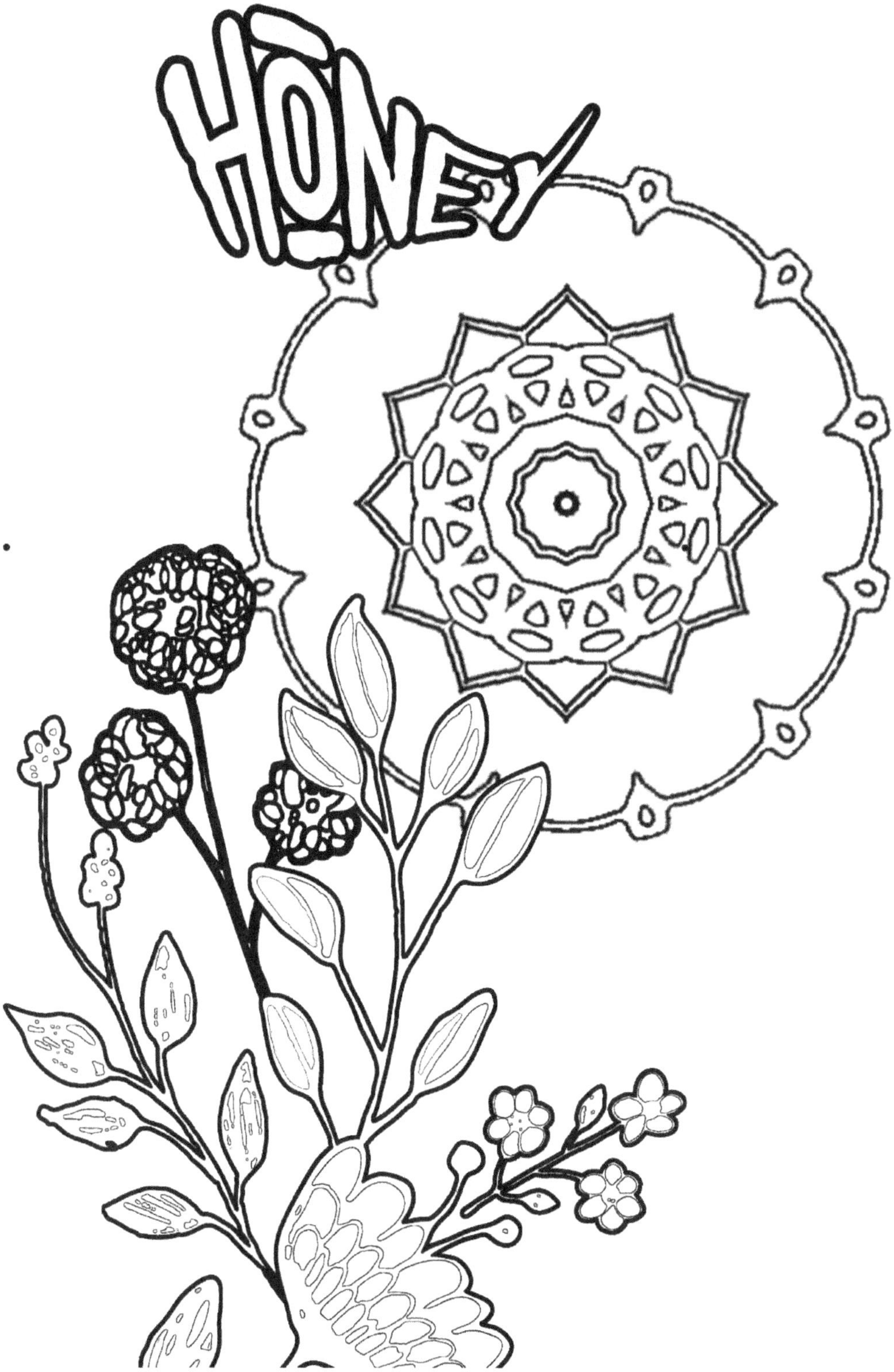
HONEY

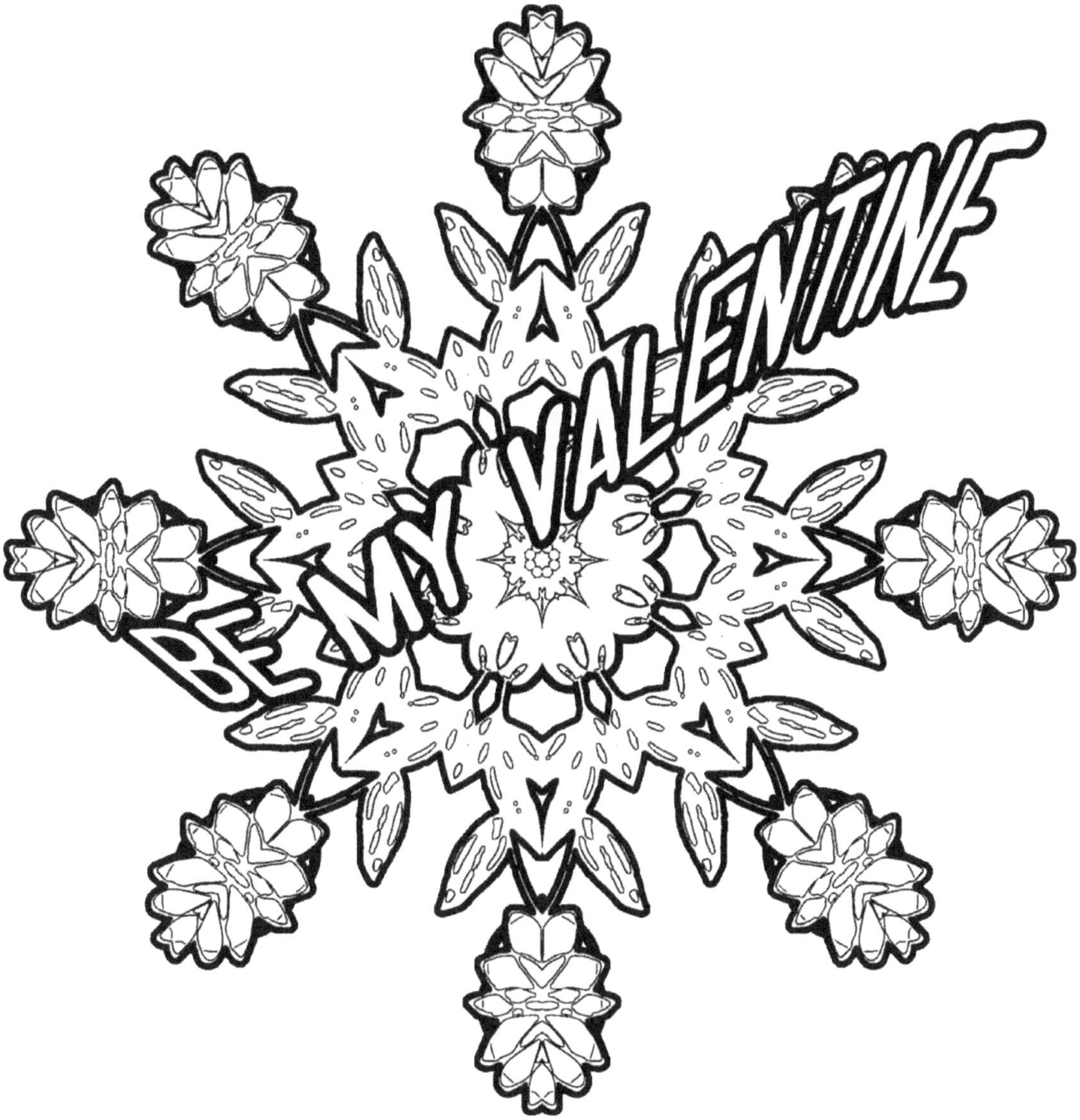
BE MY VALENTINE

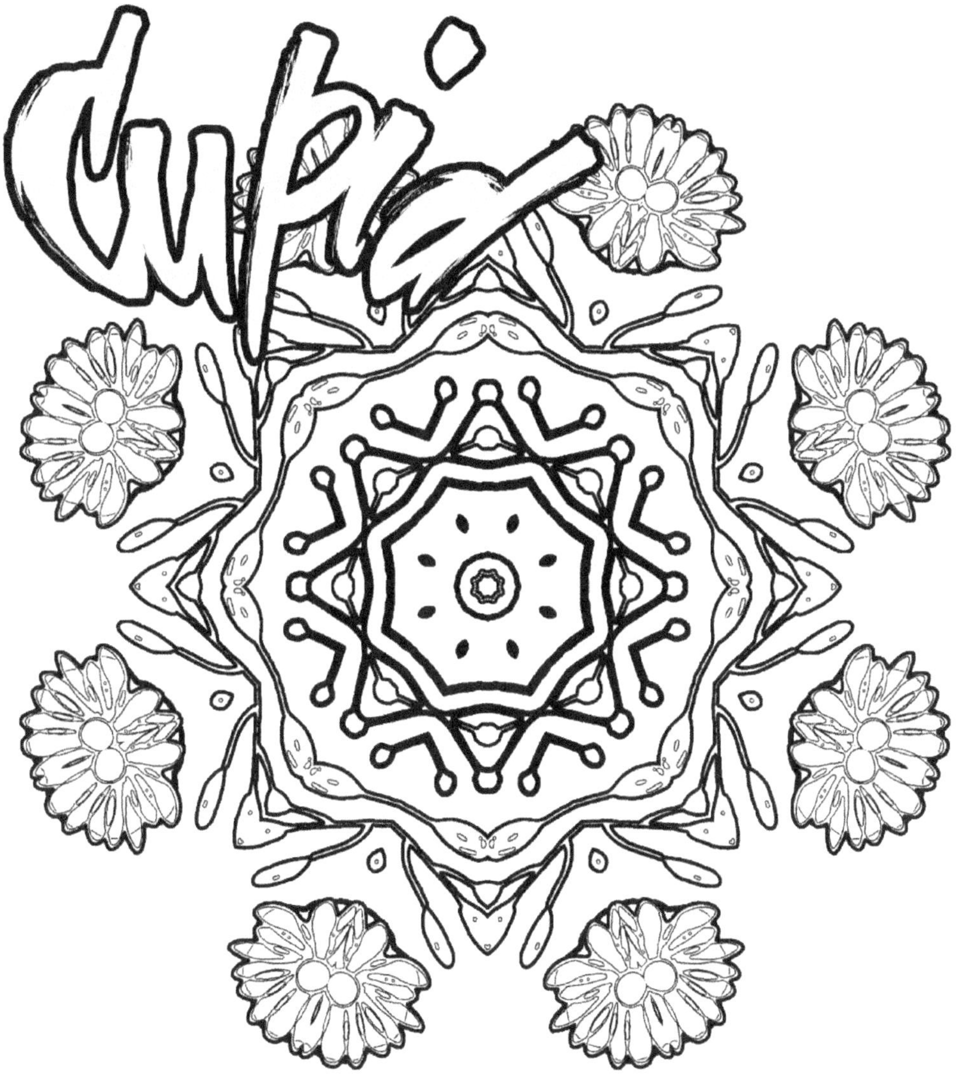
cupid

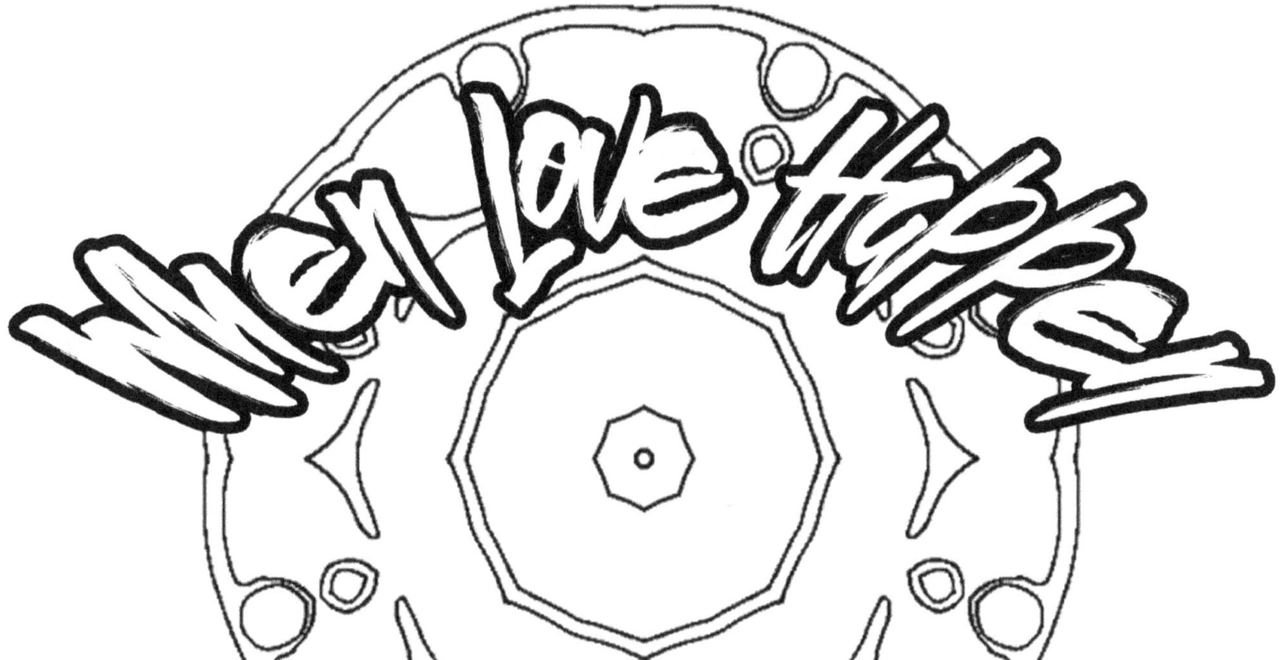
When Love Happen

WISHING YOU

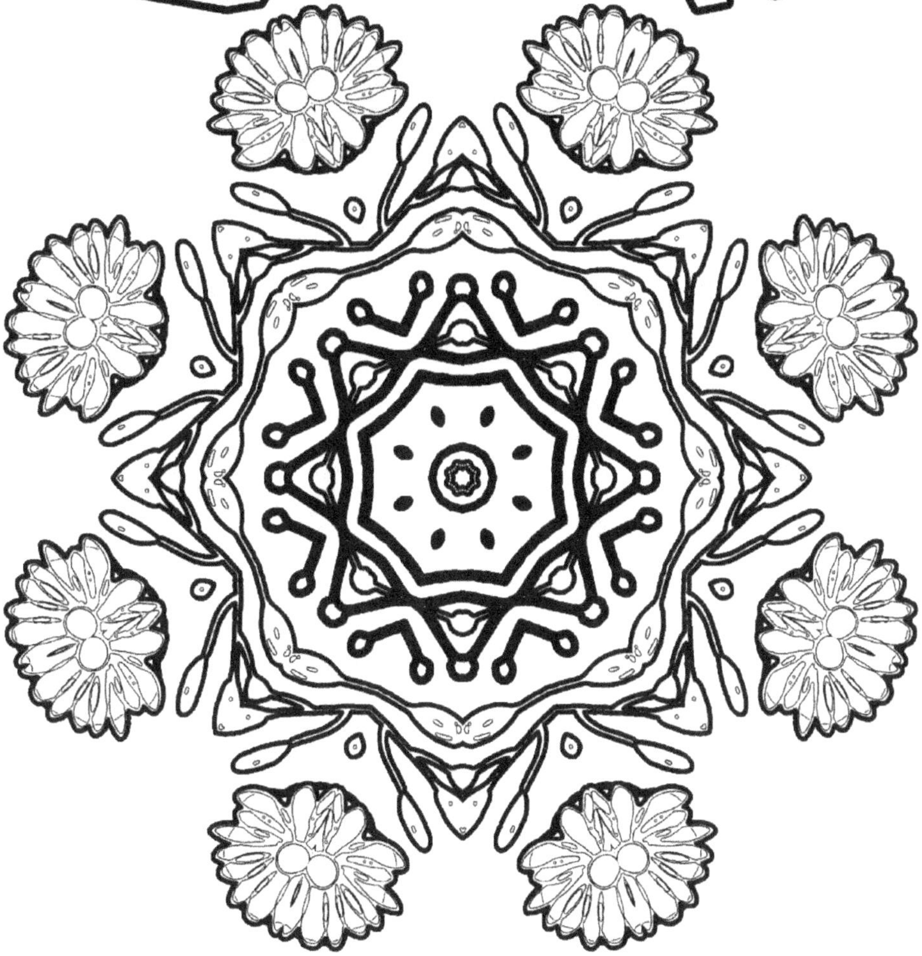

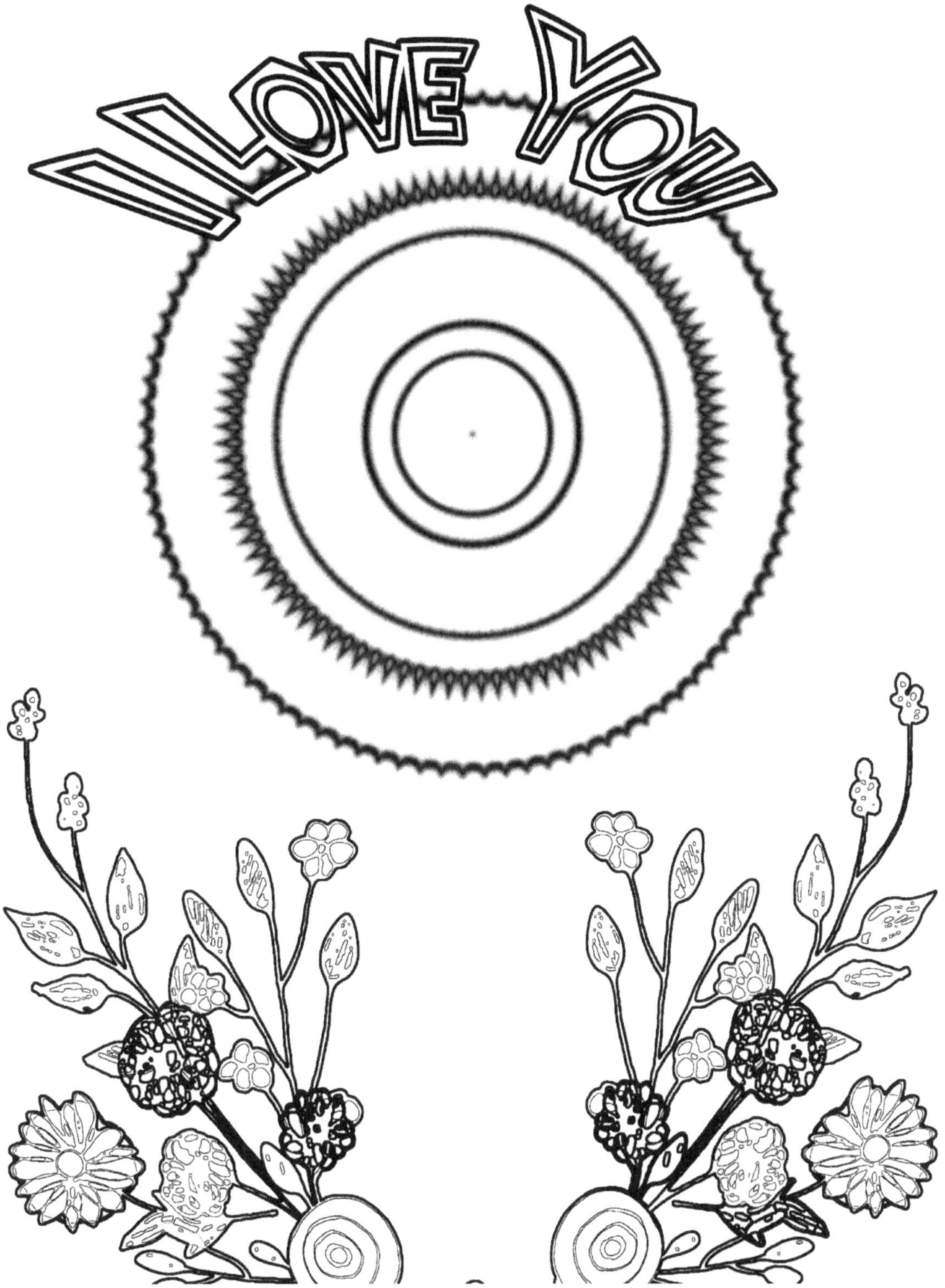
I LOVE YOU

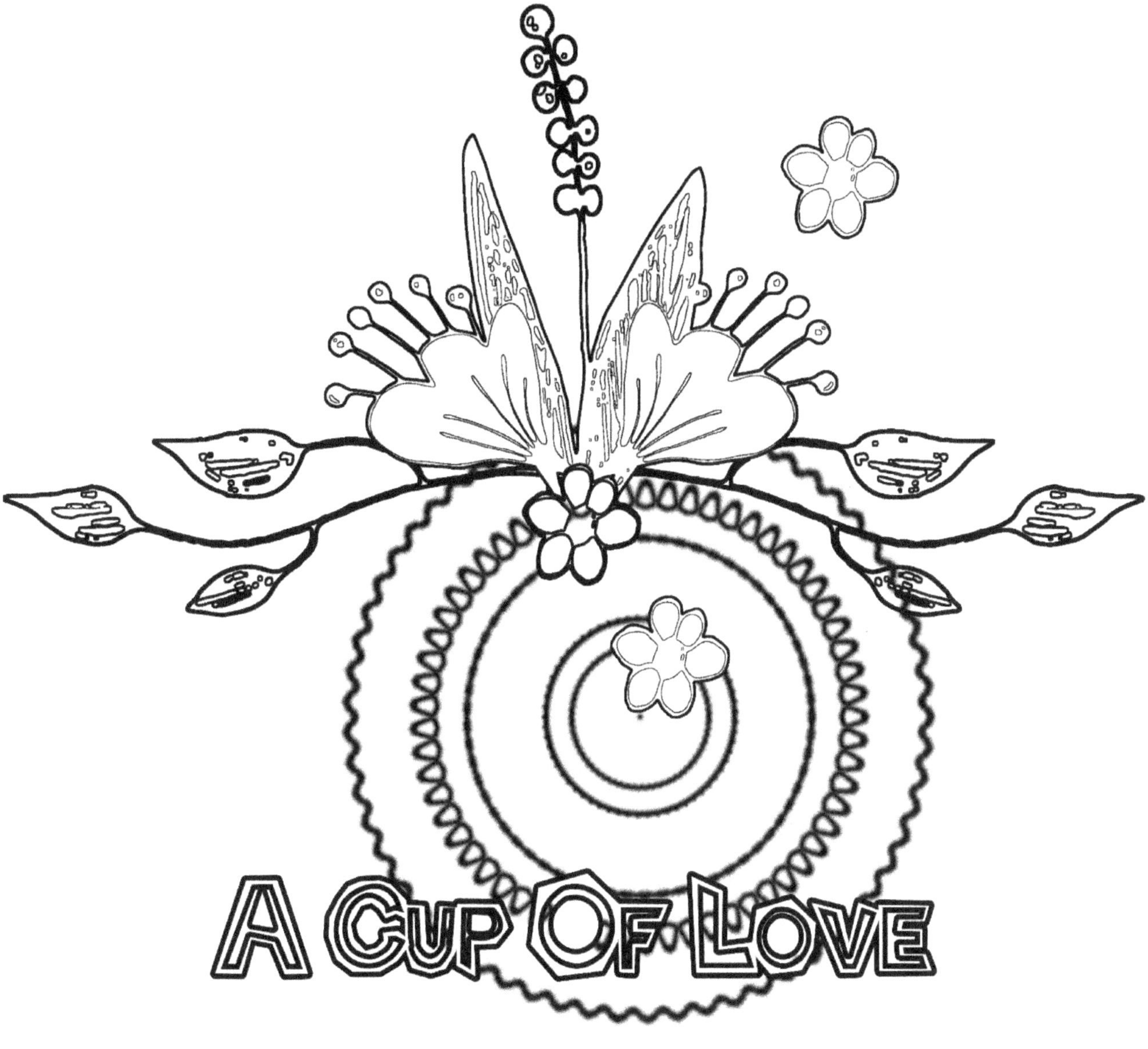
A Cup Of Love

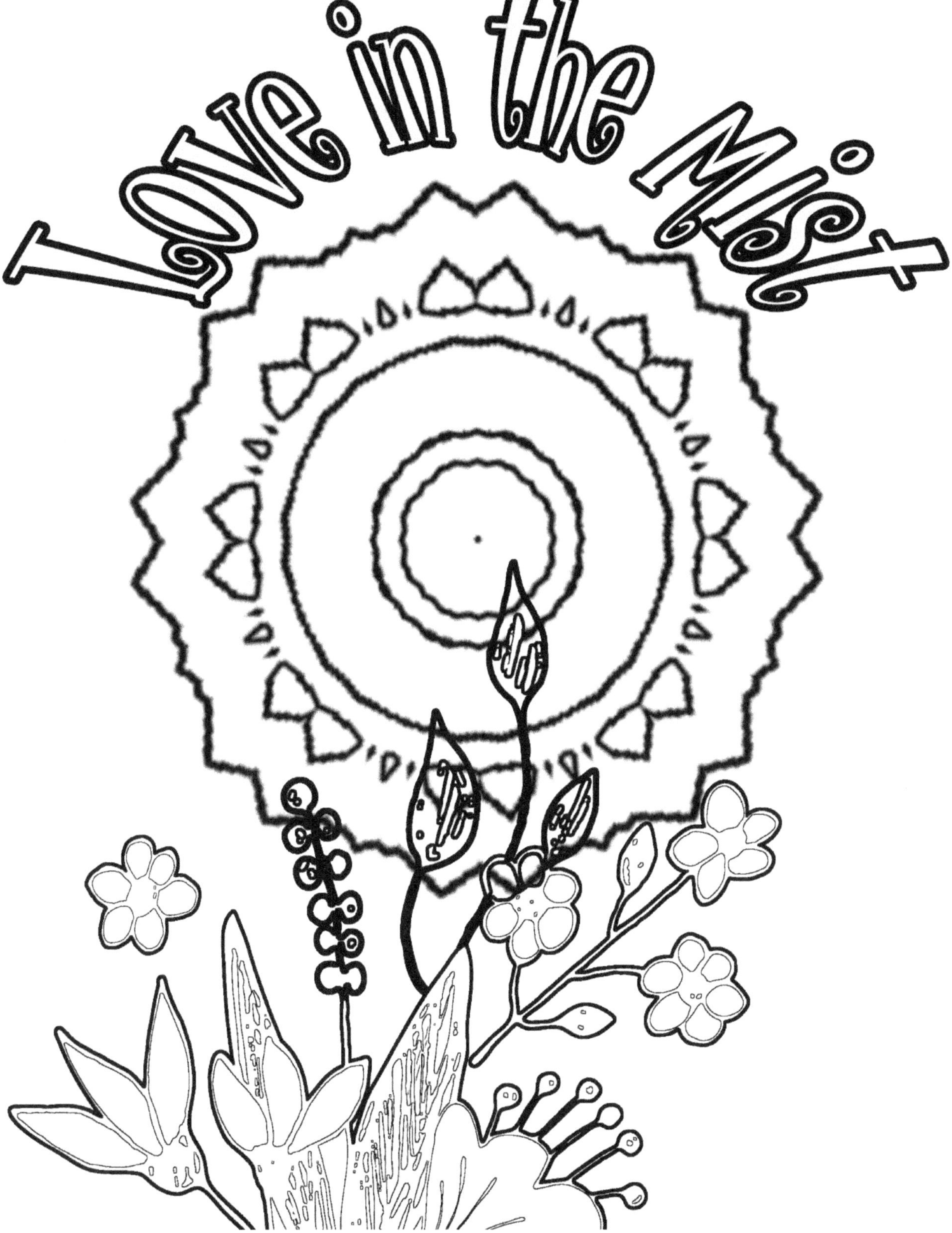
Love in the Mist

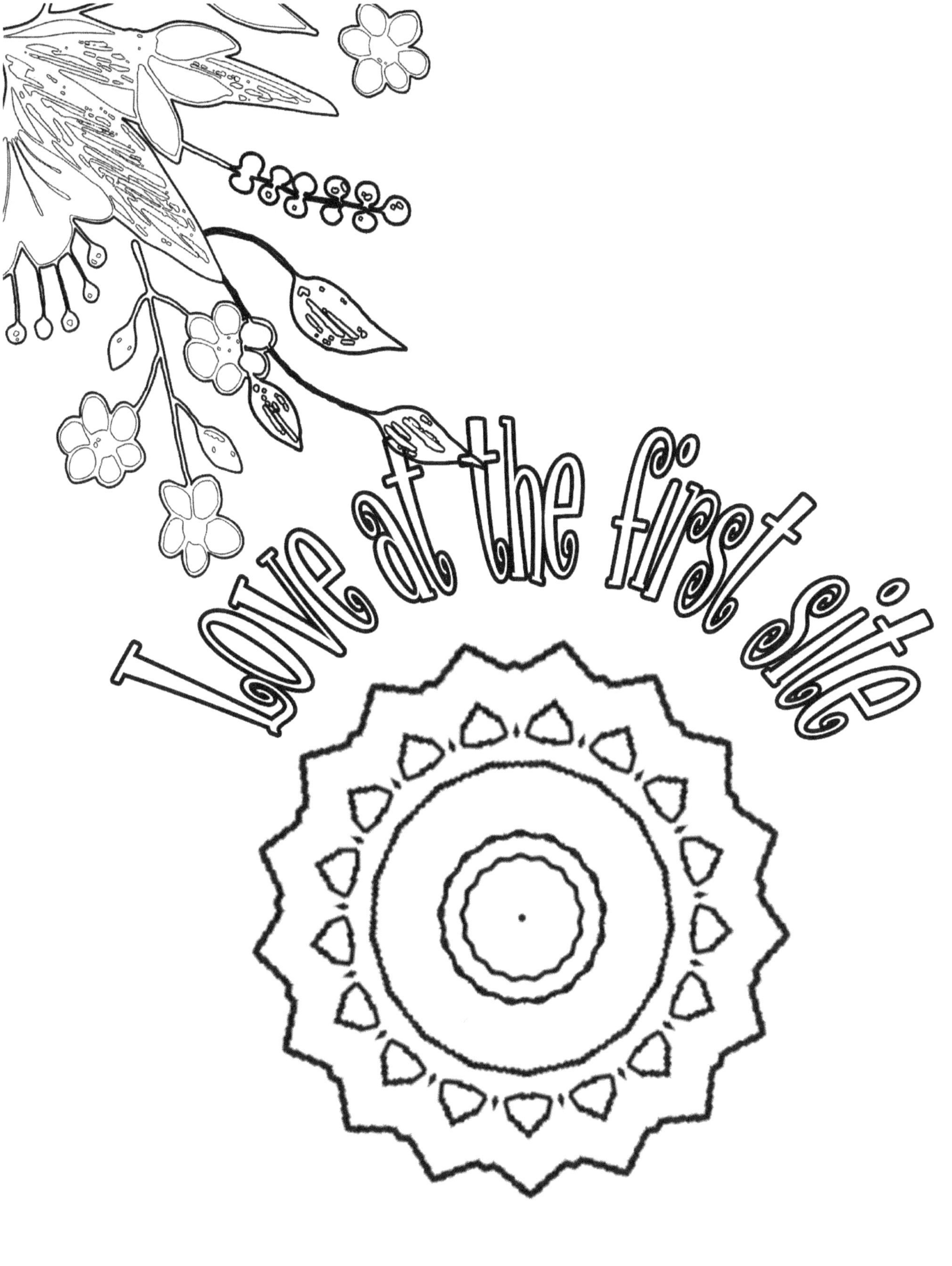
love at the first site

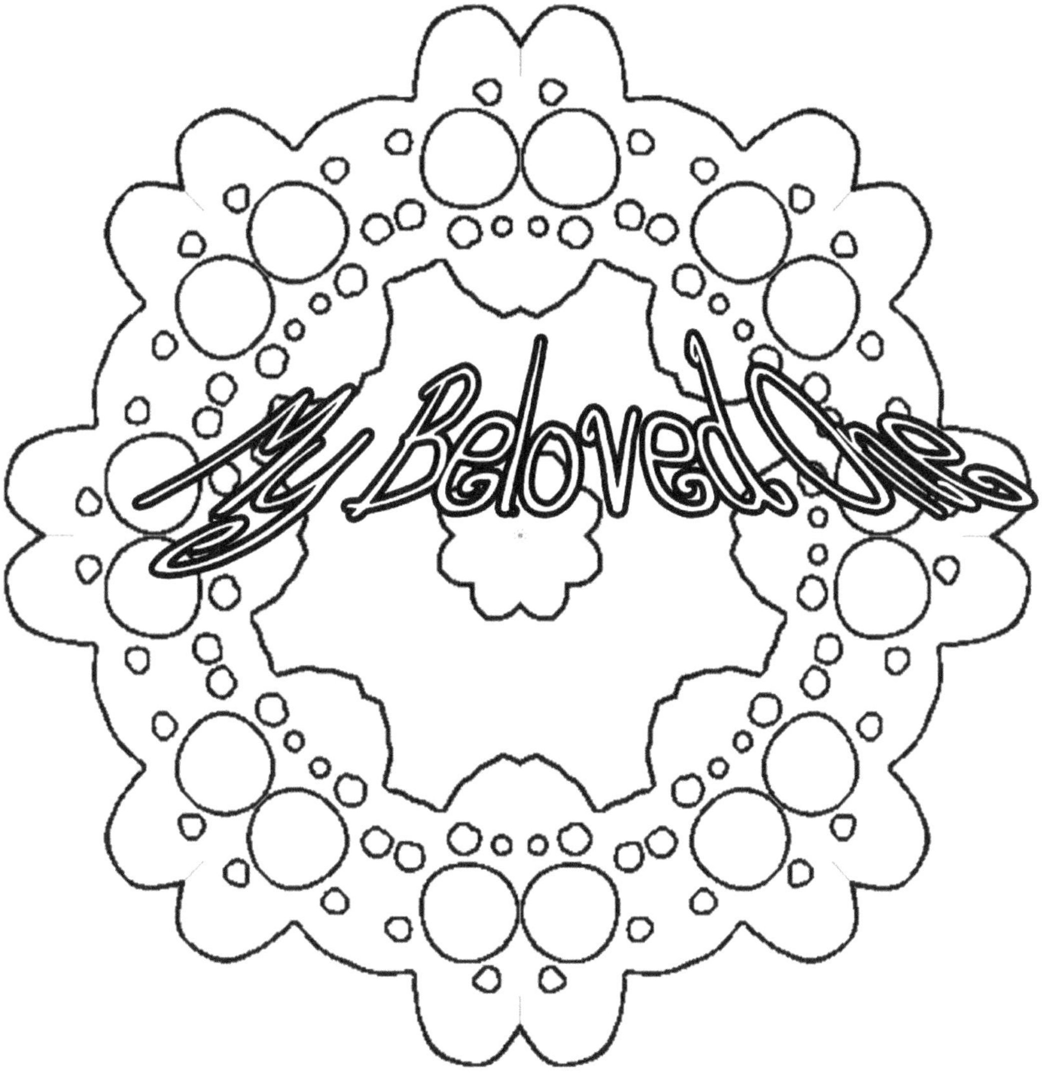
My Beloved One

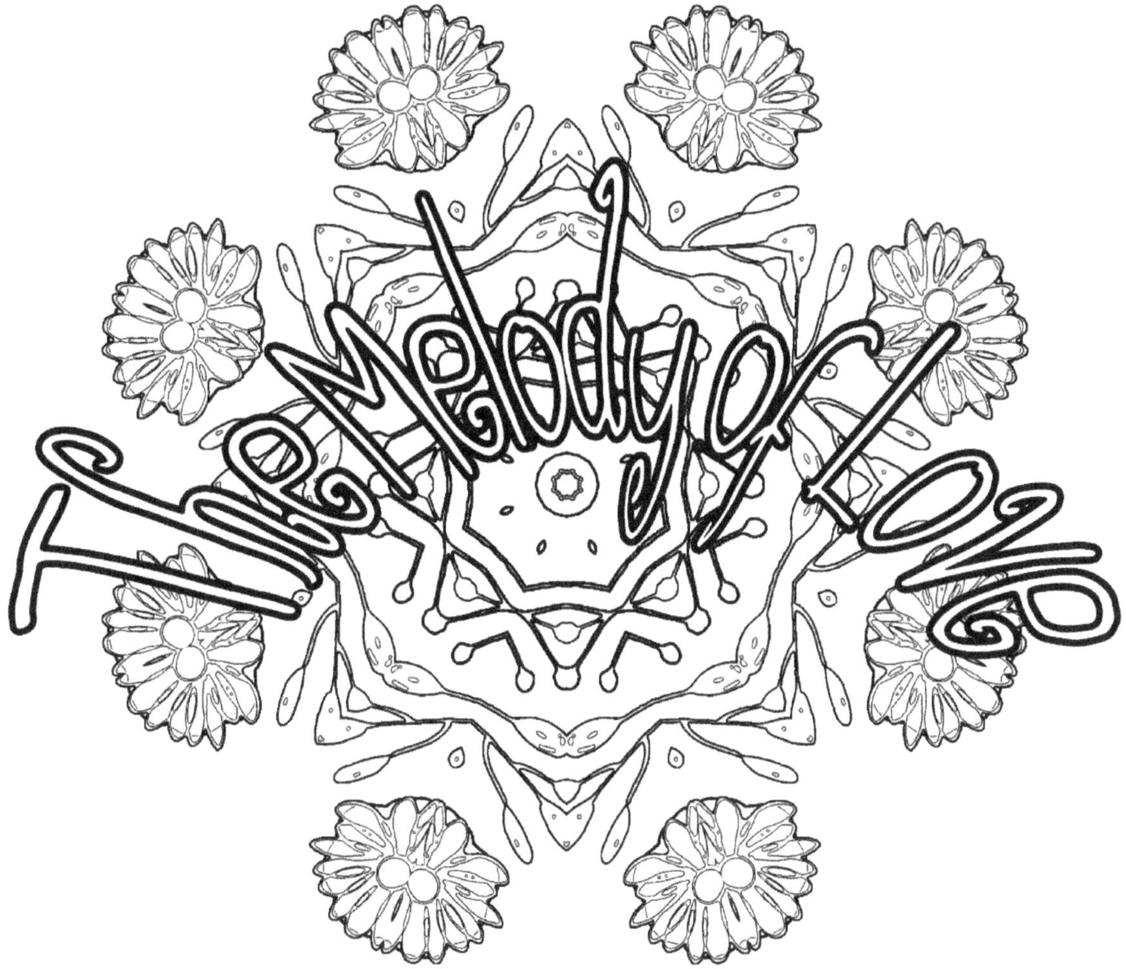
The Melody of Love

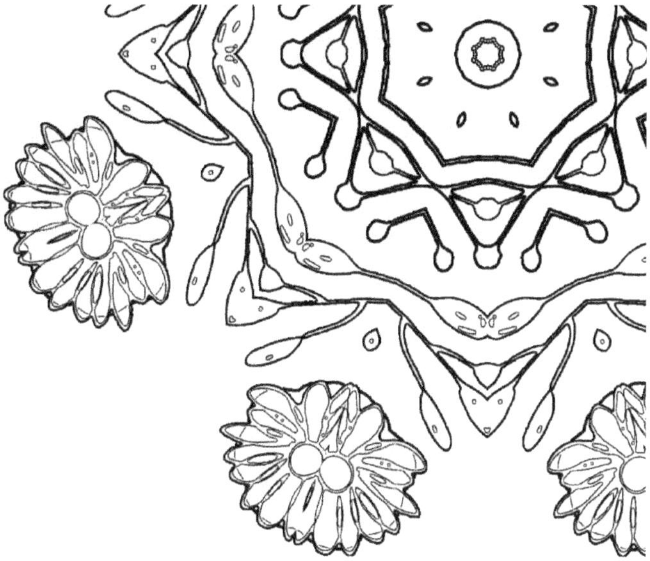

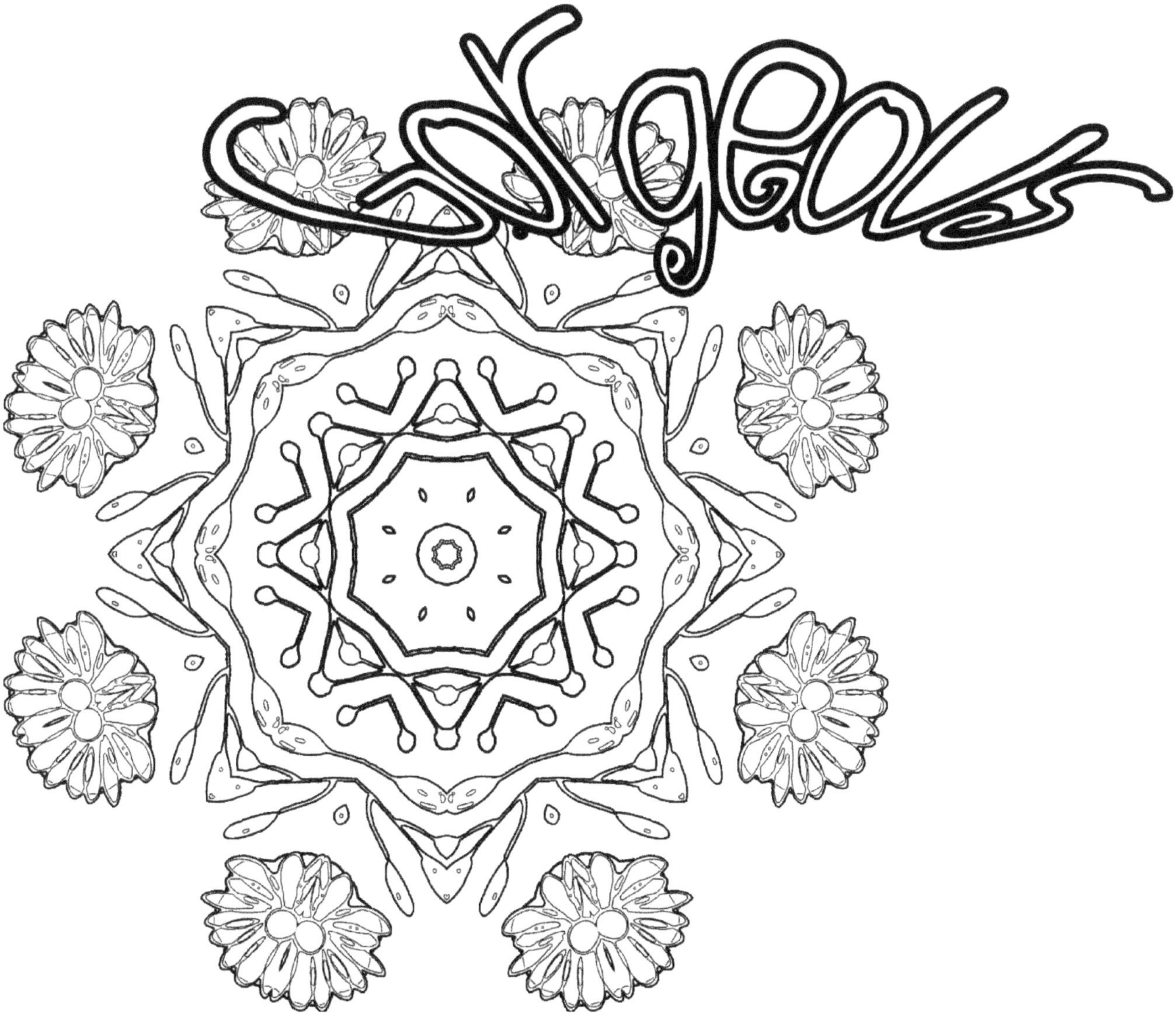

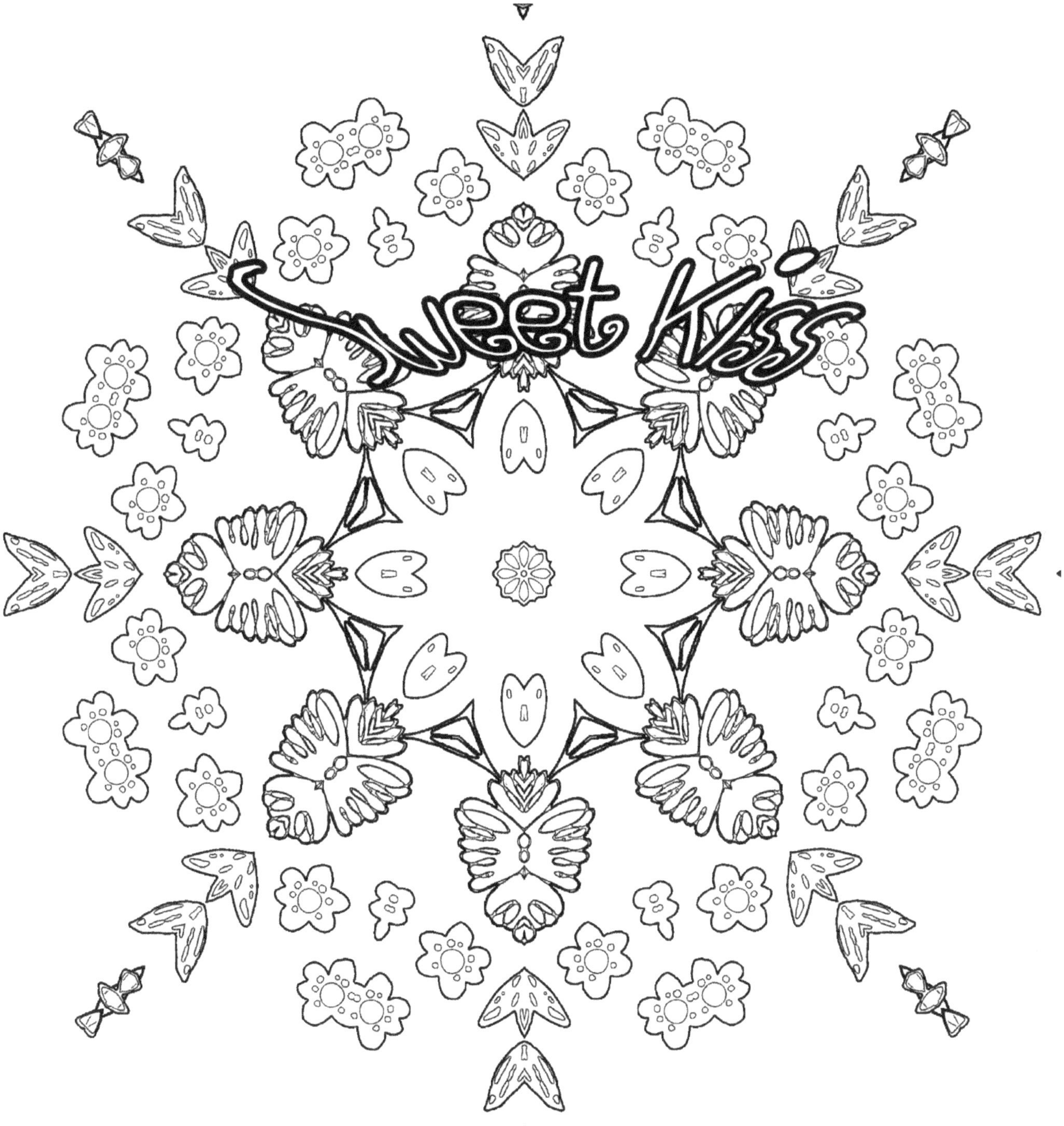
Sweet Kiss

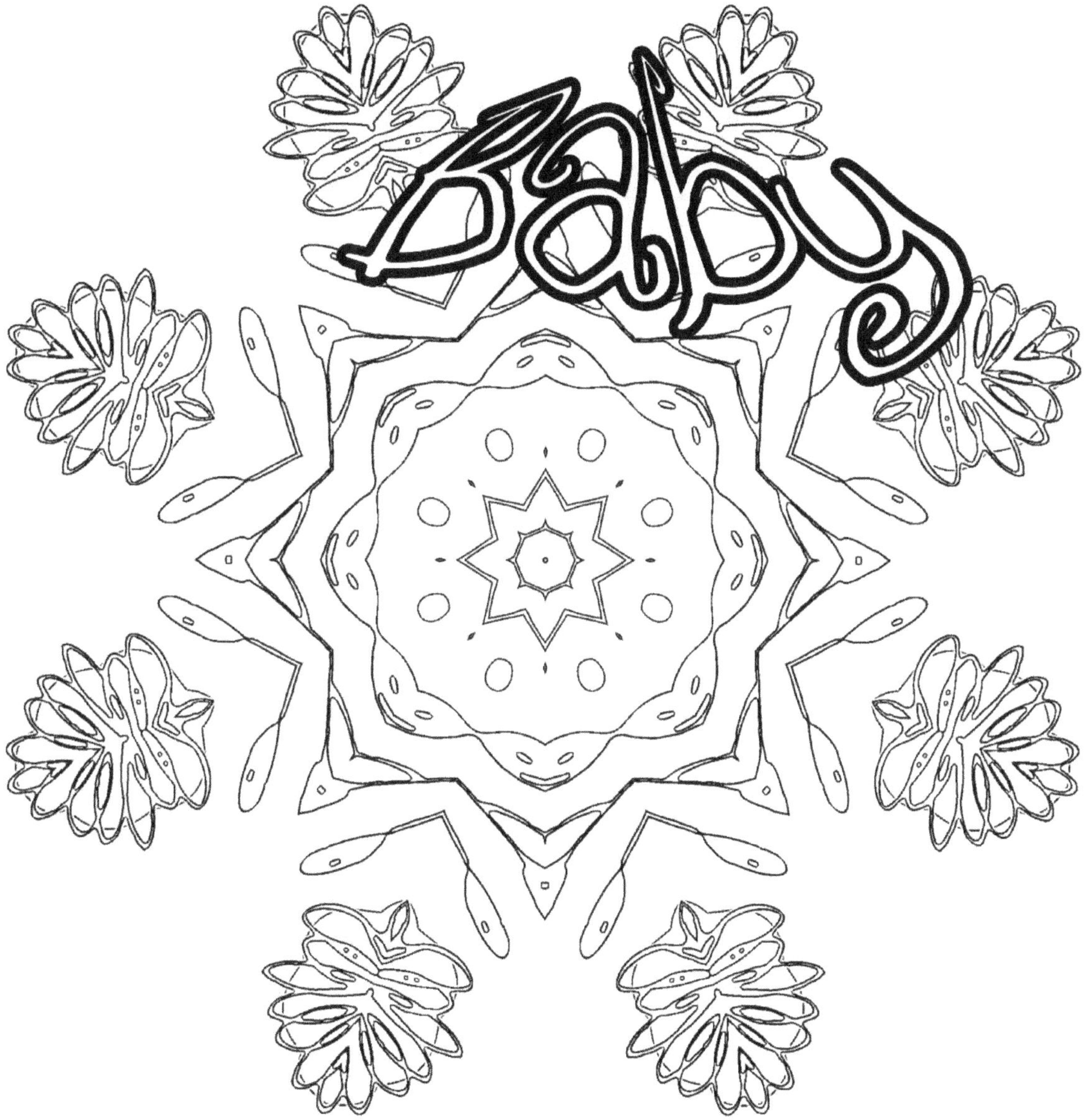
Baby

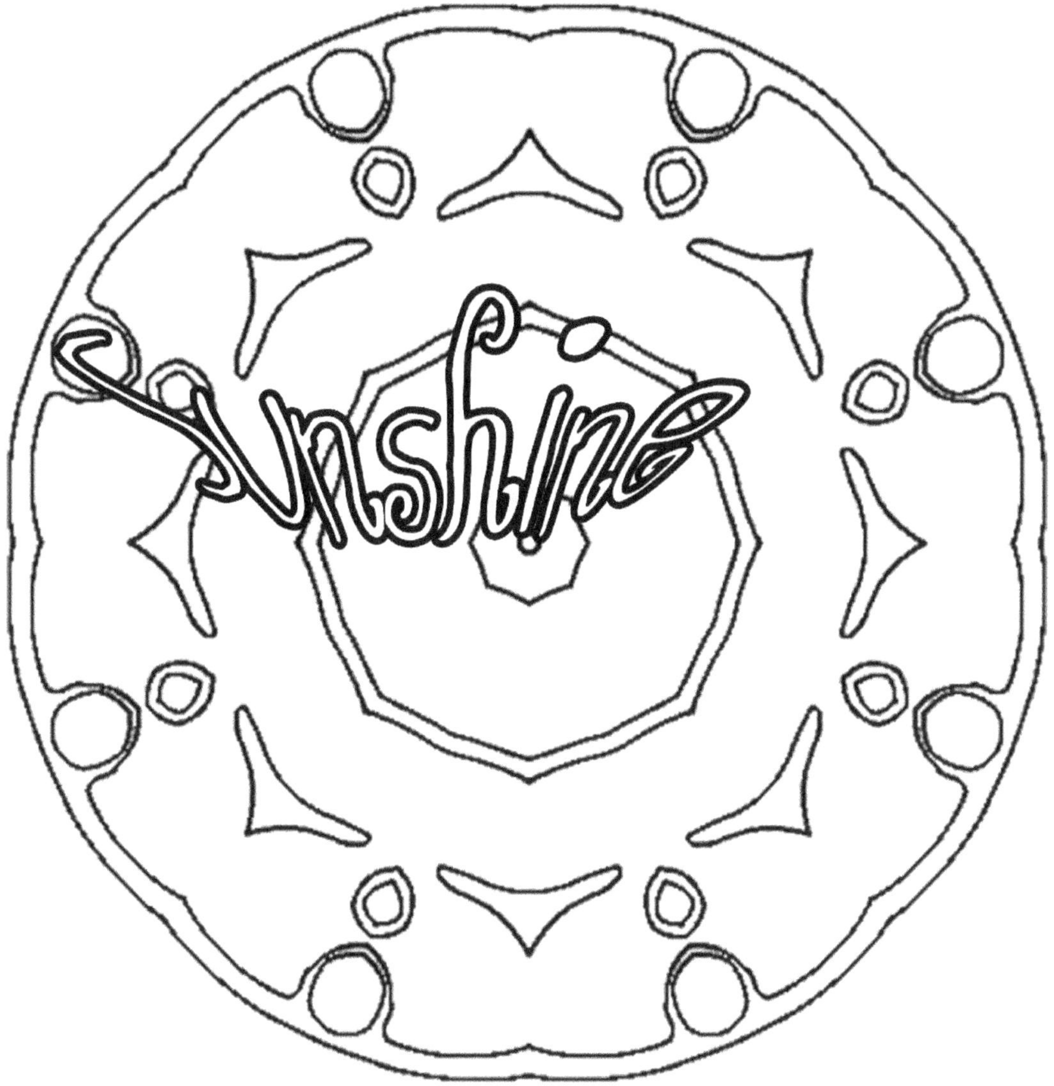
Sunshine

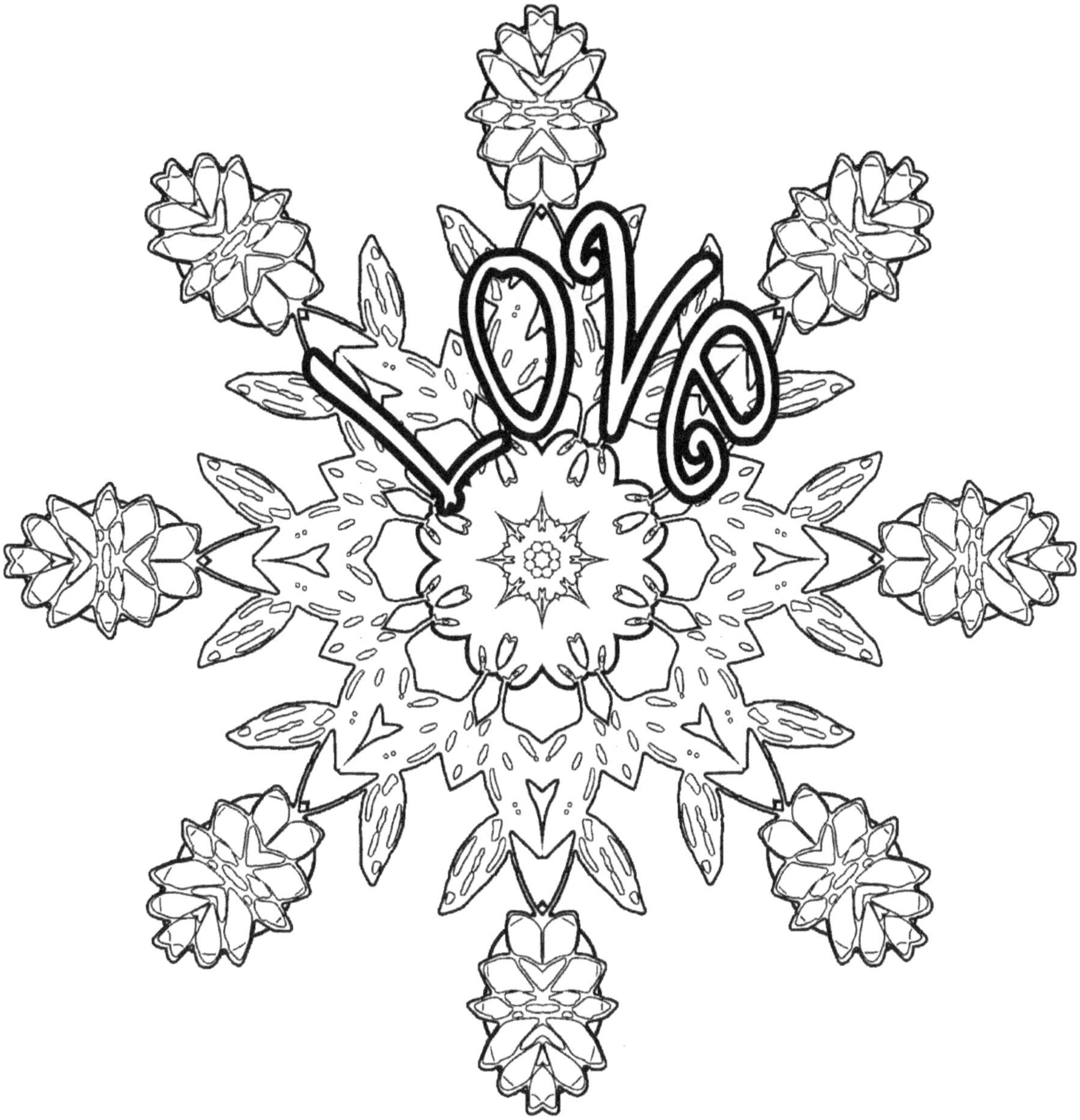
Love

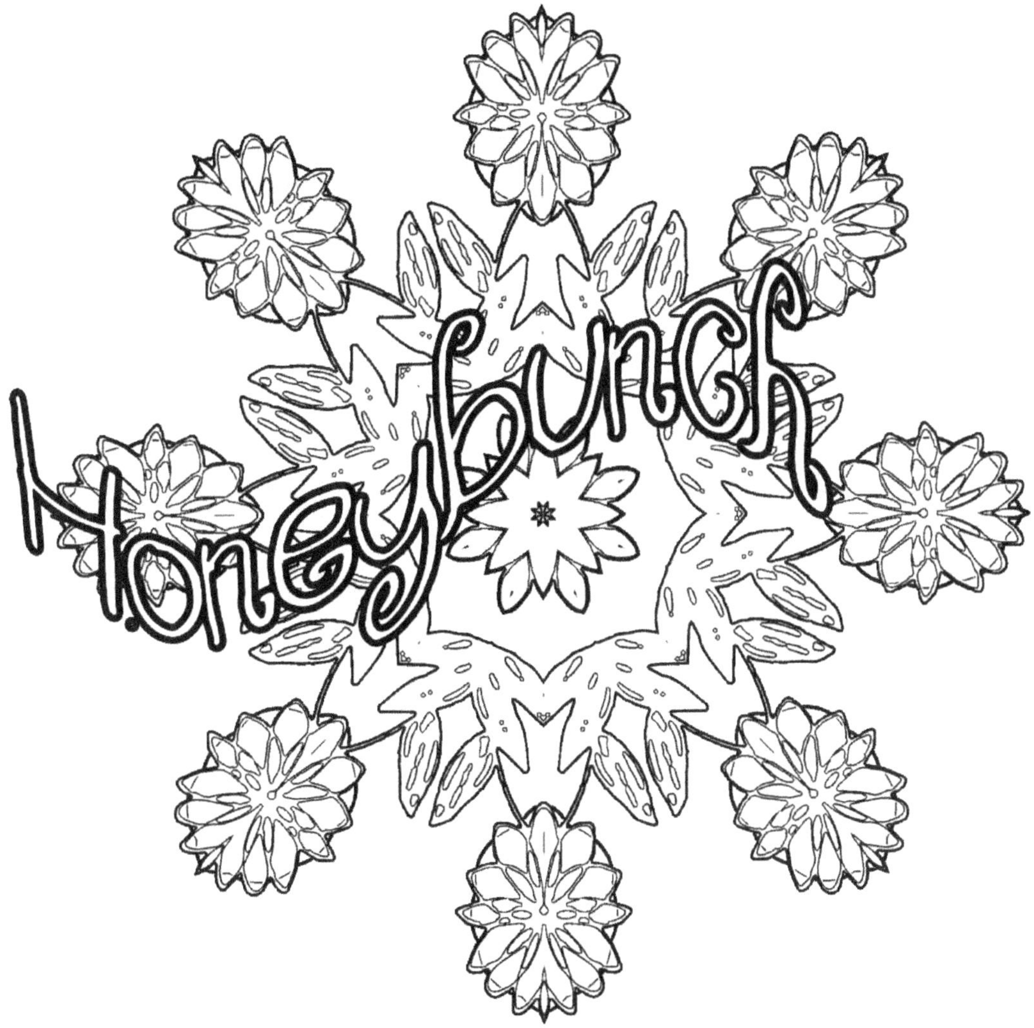
Honeybunch

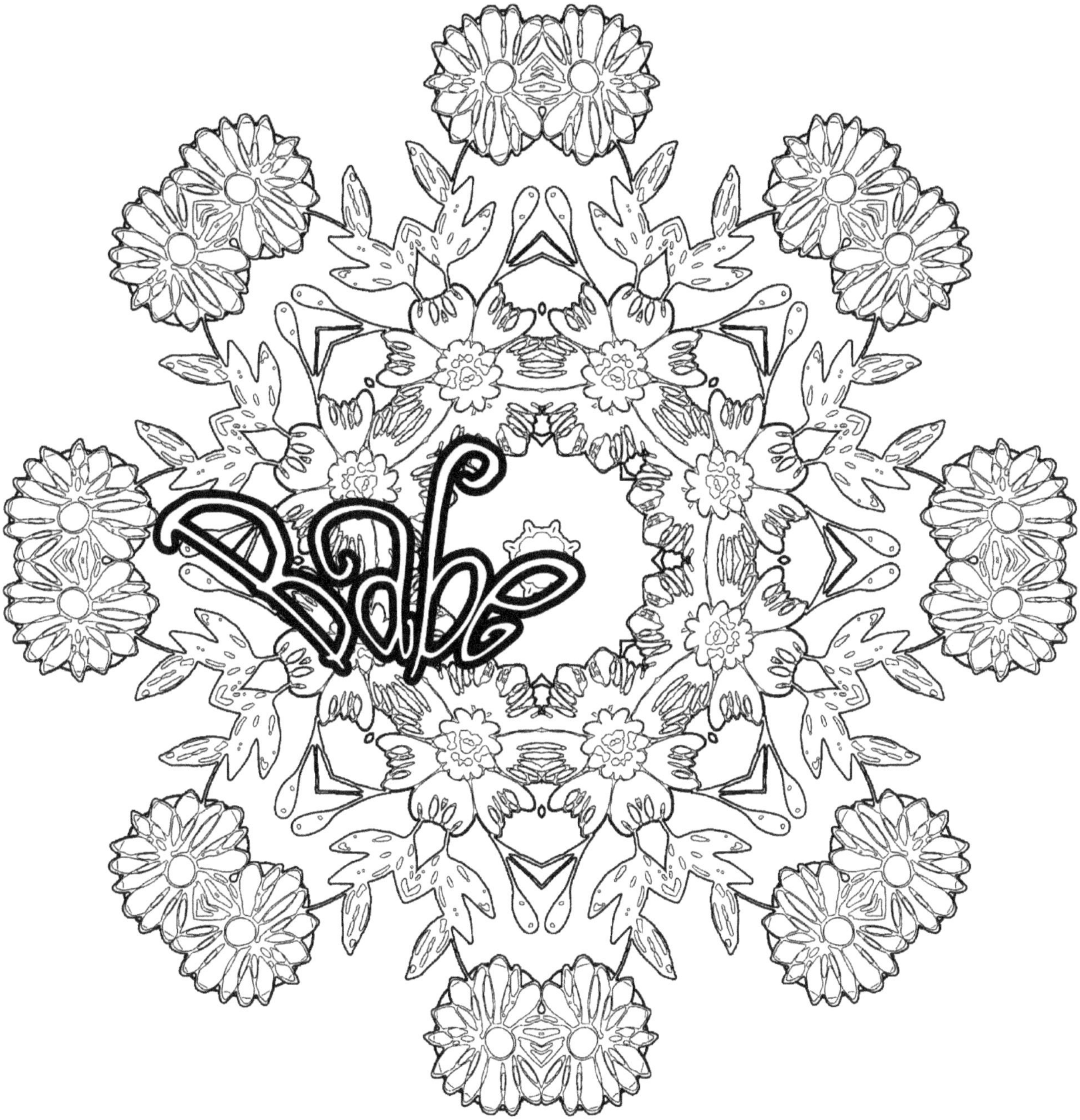
Babe

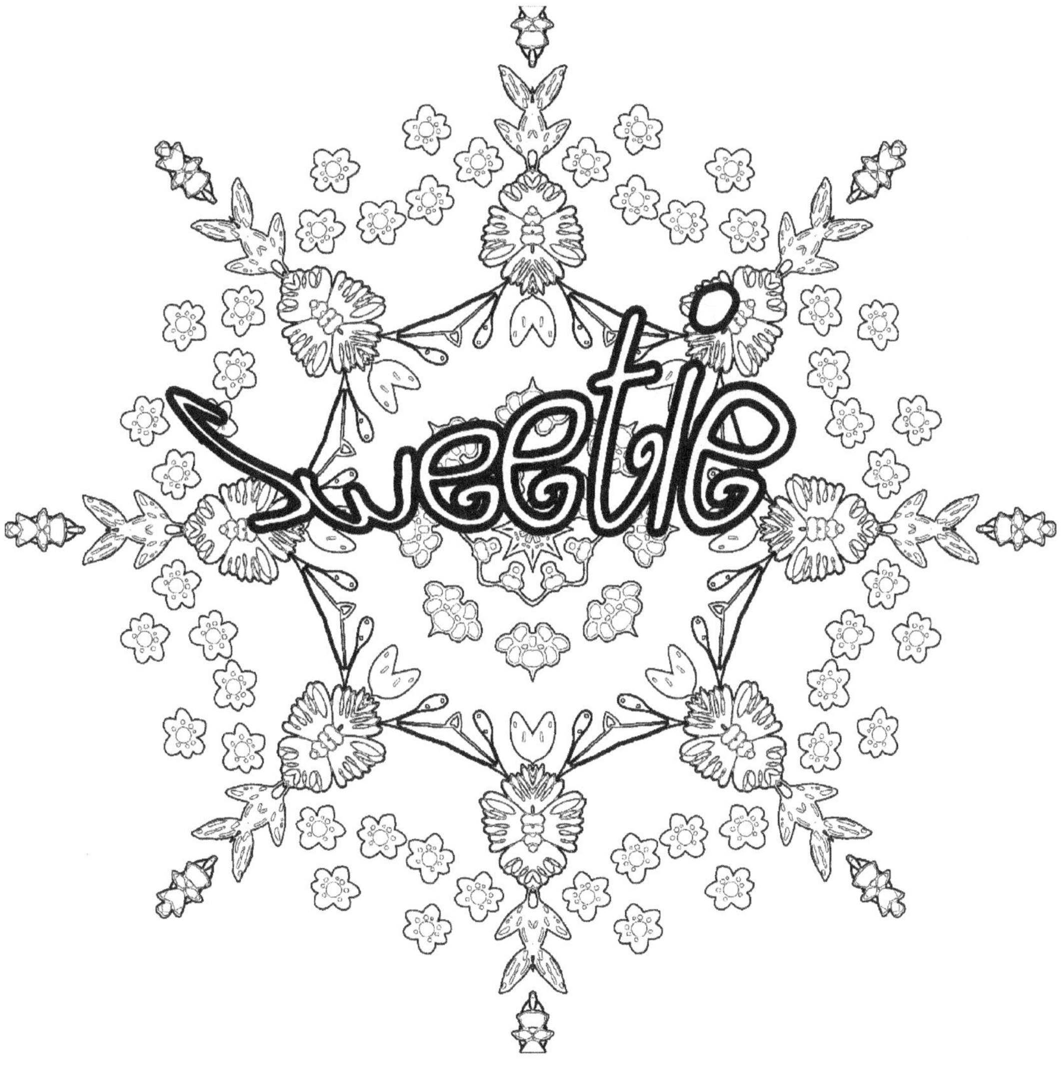
Sweetie

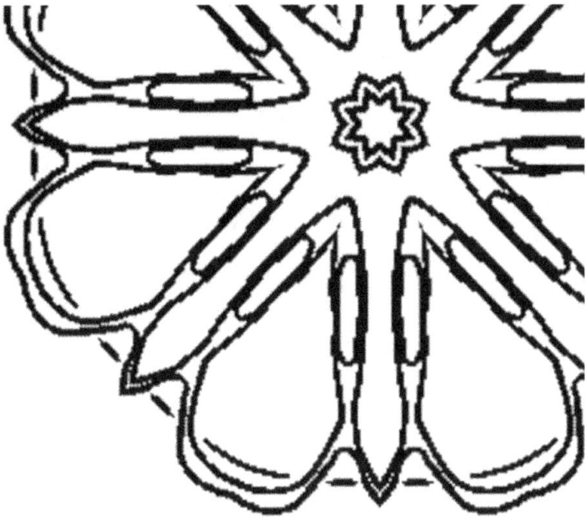

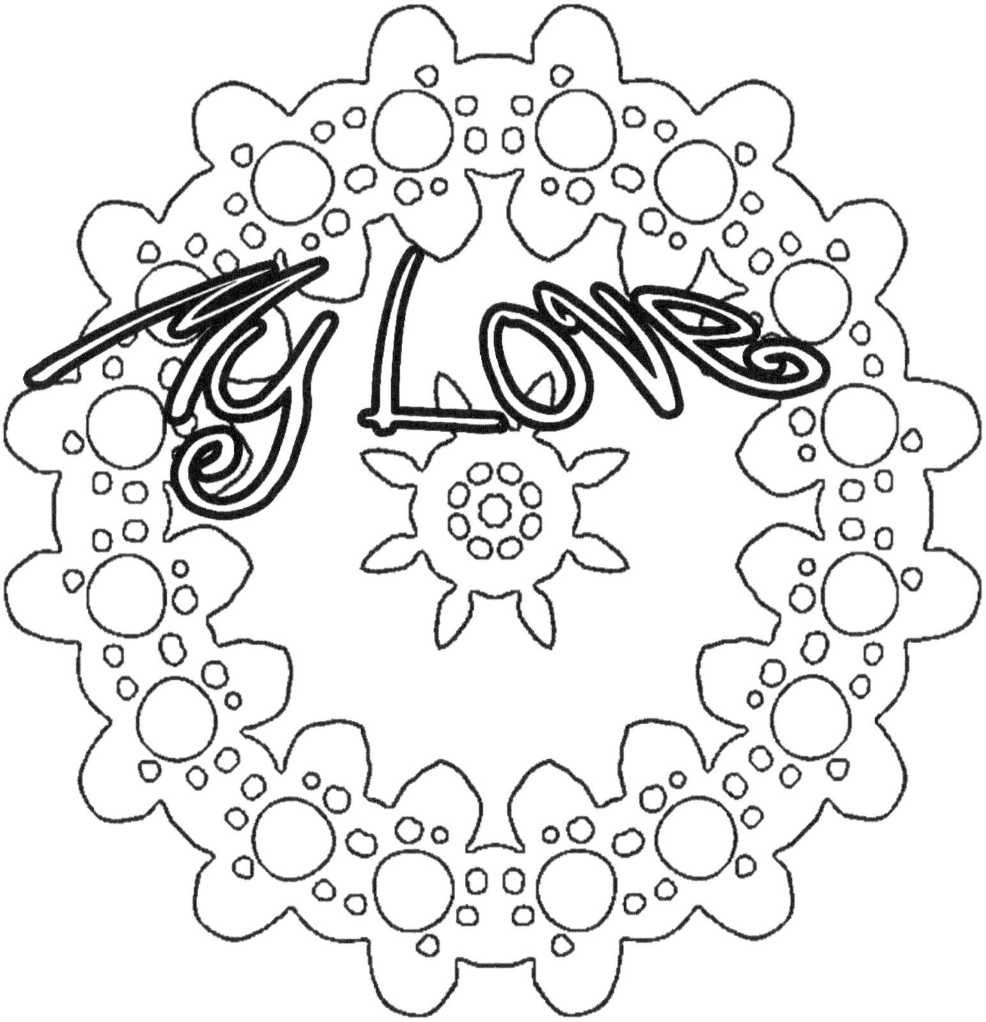
My Love

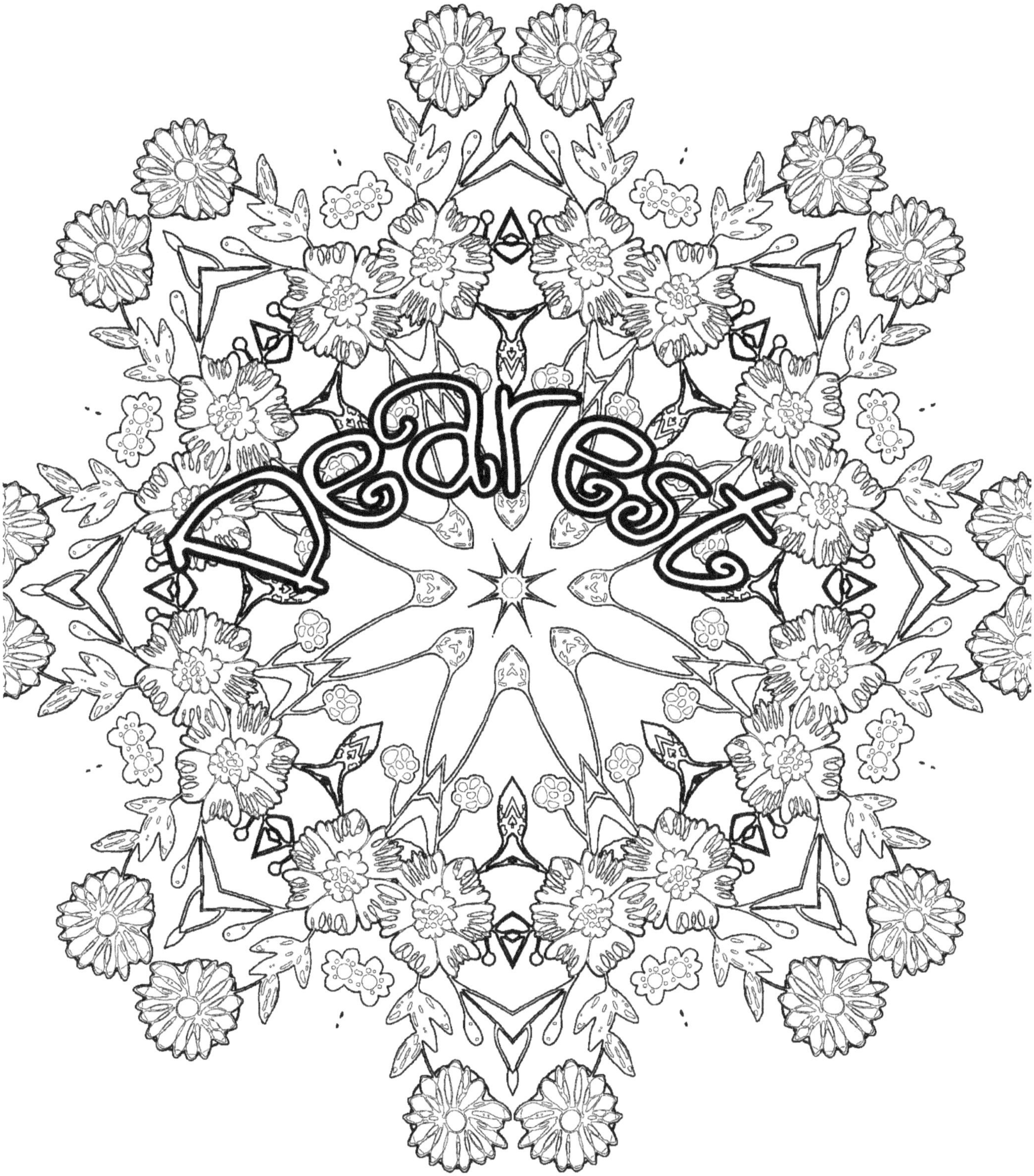
Dearest

www.ingramcontent.com/pod-product-compliance
Lightning Source LLC
Chambersburg PA
CBHW081739170526
45167CB00009B/3873
* 9 7 8 1 5 4 3 0 2 4 0 3 6 *